MODESTY

STEVE PIXLER

MODESTY

STEVE PIXLER

Published by
Continuum Ministry Resources
5200 David Strickland Rd Fort Worth TX 76119

Published in the United States by
Continuum Ministry Resources
5200 David Strickland Rd.
Fort Worth, TX 76119

Printed in the United States of America

Cover design by Derrick Pulley

ISBN13: 978-0-9796261-3-5
ISBN10: 0-9796261-3-7

Library of Congress Control Number:
2011941511

TABLE OF CONTENTS

INTRODUCTION

This book began as a series of posts on modesty that I published on my blog at stevepixler.com. The original posts are printed here largely in the same form as first published with minor editing and some expansion of chapter one. There is no doubt that this material is merely an introduction to the subject of biblical modesty. It offers a narrow perspective on what I call a "philosophy" of modesty, to use the word "philosophy" rather loosely. You will likely notice that I do not spend a great deal of time defining the particulars of specific standards of modesty, which most readers of a book like this clamor to hear. Those who peruse these pages for clear-cut rules and regulations will leave dissatisfied, and that is by deliberate design. Rule-setting is simply not my purpose here, though I do define standards of modesty quite explicitly elsewhere.

The reason for this approach is quite simple. I think we must reclaim the basic idea of modesty itself, the philosophy—or more exactly, the *theology*—of modesty. We can spend hours fussing over the details of holiness standards among ourselves, and we should do so. But we are living in a world today where modesty itself as a basic, essential Christian value has been largely rejected. This modest work— please forgive the terrible pun!—is presented to help us lay claim to the doctrine of modesty as necessary to Christian faith and life.

The world applies tremendous pressure upon our young men and women, especially our women, to abandon modesty for thoughtless public nakedness. I say "thoughtless" because most people have been dressing immodestly since childhood and simply do not think about what the exposure of their body to the public really means and what it does to their own psyche. However, when people stop to think about how they are dressing, it becomes obvious that nakedness is not natural, contrary to the naïveté of modern intellectuals who equate public nakedness with freedom and self-expression. Some "self expressions" are just better done in private.

Anyway, we shall consider various aspects of modesty in a few short chapters. There are several things that I think may help us understand better why modesty is so important. We need to develop a biblical "philosophy" of modesty so that by understanding modesty we may highly value it.

By the way, I should mention as we get started that one of the best books on modesty I have read is *Christian Modesty and the Public Undressing of America* by Jeff Pollard. Great book. You may also want to read *A Return to Modesty* by Wendy Shalit. A modern Jewish perspective on modesty can be found in *Modesty: An Adornment for Life* by Rabbi Falk.

There are countless other books available, and I think we should read them all. For too long this subject has been pushed to the perimeter of Christian thought, and it is time to bring it back to the essential center where it belongs. Modesty is not a fringe issue. It is central to the Christian faith and the coming of Christ's kingdom in the earth. May God grant us the wisdom and courage to restore biblical teaching on modesty to the church of Jesus Christ.

CHAPTER ONE

MODESTY AND SCRIPTURE

I should begin by saying that we should practice modesty in dress styles for no other reason than the fact that God told us to do so. We are commanded to "dress with modest apparel" in I Timothy 2, and this apostolic command flows out of the long tradition of Old Testament holiness teaching. The word "modest" in I Timothy 2 means "well arranged" clothing, which, read together with the rest of the text, certainly means that we should wear clothing that covers our nakedness.

The idea of modest clothing as a necessity of propriety begins with the beginning of human history. In the Garden of Eden, God clothed Adam and Eve in garments of animal skins after they sinned and were discovered partially dressed in aprons, or "loin cloths" (ESV), made of fig leaves. The Lord God also had much to say throughout the Law and the Prophets on the topic of nakedness and the shame of public exposure. The simple fact that God forbade us to look on the nakedness of another man's wife should be reason enough to preach strong sermons against the tendency of pagan culture to undress in public. And that would be anywhere in public, including the public pool or beach. There are no exceptions. God condemns the practice of running naked in the streets.

This means that we should dress modestly whether or not we understand the theology of modesty. In other words, we should do so just because "the Bible tells us so." Moreover, we should seek to define modesty by Scripture and not by surrounding culture. We must look for biblical definitions of modesty. Now this quest may produce some minor variations as we attempt to reach a consensus on particular standards of modesty because the Bible does not offer fully explicit guidelines for how we should dress. The Ten Commandments do not include stipulations on how long a skirt must be or how high a neckline must be. "Thou shalt not wear a miniskirt" simply does not appear there. The Law says nothing about sleeve length or two-piece bathing suits. The Word of God simply does not address modesty with this sort of detail. Yet, we cannot deny that God commands us to cover our nakedness. So, defining nakedness, and thus, defining modesty, is a necessary task.

I think we should at least all agree that the Bible does present basic outlines for modesty. As noted above, it seems that the Lord God established a sort of modesty baseline in the Garden of Eden when He clothed Adam and Eve in robes ("coats" – KJV) to cover their nakedness. It seems that Adam and Eve's fashionable fig leaves did not cover enough skin to satisfy the Creator. And it also seems reasonable to me, to exercise a little theological extrapolation, that the garments with which God clothed Adam and Eve would have at least covered the upper arms, torso, bosom, back and thighs. The aprons they crafted covered their midriff, and God still considered them naked. So it seems to me that God's *haute couture* would have covered what a robe would cover. Indeed, these robes that God designed from skins seem to have set the pattern for the way much of the world has dressed since that time.

This gives rise to the idea—a reasonable idea, in my opinion—that the robes in Eden should provide for us a threshold standard for modesty. I like to call this the "robe standard." Paul looked back to the beginning to discover creation ordinances when teaching on the proper roles of men and women in the church (I Corinthians 11; I Timothy 2), and we should not hesitate to follow his example. We should never accept a definition of modesty that does not at least seek to conform to this creation ordinance.

In our church, as a very conservative, holiness-tradition Pentecostal church, we interpret this robe standard to mean that we should wear clothing with sleeves covering the upper arms; with high necklines that cover the bosom completely; no backless garments; and clothing that cover the thighs altogether, which, in a practical sense, works out to mean garments at least below the knees whether standing or seated. We also teach that clothing should not immodestly "expose" the body by "accentuating rather than hiding the graceful curves" (as Wodehouse would say) of the form and figure.

Now, this may seem way too conservative for some and far too liberal for others, which is, of course, why I am not taking the time here to argue the point any further. However, I think, generally speaking, most of us who are sincerely seeking a biblical definition of modesty would not argue much with this basic outline of modesty. And those who are *not* seeking a biblical definition of modesty are not going to listen to anything we have to say, anyhow. They are too busy getting naked in public.

Beyond all the finicky details, my point is simply this: God requires us to dress modestly, and the Bible must define what that means.

CHAPTER TWO

MODESTY AND MATURITY

One of the great lessons that we must learn about modesty is the fact that modesty is a mark of maturity, while nakedness, and I mean the public display of nakedness, is a mark of immaturity. In the very young, or the newly created, like Adam and Eve, nakedness is a mark of innocence. We think nothing of nakedness in those who themselves think nothing of nakedness because they are too young to know better. When they streak through the front yard, we just laugh and scoop them up in our arms and take them quickly inside. If our middle-aged neighbor tries that, we will call the police. And they will scoop him up in the awful grip of the law, to again quote Wodehouse, without even the hint of a smile.

The fact that Adam and Eve were "naked and not ashamed" has led some people to the false conclusion that nakedness is the ideal creation state. Nudists are famous for this misunderstanding, though they probably do not refer often to scripture to make their point. However, nudists notwithstanding, a closer look at scripture reveals that God never intended for Adam and Eve to remain unclothed.

For example, a quick look in the Book of Revelation at the final, eternal state of resurrected man shows that man's ultimate destiny is to be clothed in robes of righteousness, and this is not just bare metaphor, no pun intended.

God left Adam and Eve naked at first because they were just married and alone in their leafy, honeymoon suite. There were lessons about intimacy that God planned to teach the giggling newlyweds, and that sort of thing requires glorious nakedness. We shall talk more on modesty and intimacy later.

However, the point to be emphasized here is that nakedness was a temporary state. God had always planned to clothe Adam and Eve as He fellowshipped with them in daily communion and brought them into the rank and responsibility of dominion over creation. And the idea of rank and responsibility is fundamentally associated with clothing. As with Joseph's coat of many colors, clothing represents rank and position. Clothing manifests power and prestige. This is true in every walk of life and in every culture. We expect people to dress befitting their station in life.

Barbarians and savages run naked in the jungle, but civilized people put on clothes. As cultures mature, they get dressed. This is because of the direct creational connection between modesty and maturity. This idea may be often suppressed in our neo-pagan culture, but it is rooted deep in our psyche, and we cannot escape it. The return of our culture to casual, thoughtless public nudity is an indication of our decline back into slavish barbarity, not an indication of our advance into liberated enlightenment.

And as a side note, the recent popularity of tattoos and piercings reveal the same steady decline into slavery. Free people resist being branded like cattle. Slaves meekly acquiesce. To be branded is to be owned, like gang members, like their girlfriends, like pirates, prison inmates and all those other wannabe rebels desperately seeking to display individuality by doing what everyone around them is doing.

From my perspective, tattoos are boring symbols of mindless conformity. If you really want to be an individual, put on a suit and tie and dress with a little class. My once conformist business suit is the new symbol of countercultural defiance. I am the reckless libertine! Read it and weep, all you lemmings.

Seriously now, for those who are getting stamped, branded and engraved, who owns you?

The bottom line is this. Modesty reveals a respect for who we are and for others around us. This self-respect comes as we grow in a mature awareness of others. Every mom learns this as she tries to teach her three-year-old his table manners. To be unaware and unashamed of nakedness is to demonstrate an immature lack of appreciation for the image of God that we were created to display. We are destined to rule the world, and we would look pretty silly on the throne in our birthday suit. When we dress immodestly, we betray contempt for our position.

CHAPTER THREE

MODESTY AND INTIMACY

One of the deepest desires of the human heart is to experience intimacy. Intimacy is an aspect of love, for intimacy is the mutual sharing of self that only occurs in true love. We often think of love as being purely selfless service, but there is much more to love than this. Love that seeks only the satisfaction of others is actually self-love twisted into masochistic self-loathing. Love not only seeks to satisfy others by serving their genuine needs (though not necessarily all their wants), but love also seeks to find satisfaction for self in such selfless service. In other words, love seeks mutual satisfaction, which is existential fulfillment, and this sort of mutual self-realization is intimacy.

Intimacy requires secrecy. In order to truly experience intimacy we must share relationship in a mutually inclusive and exclusive way. There must be boundaries. We must shut some people in and some people out in order to experience intimacy. All healthy relationships entail this polar balance of mutual inclusivity and exclusivity.

The parent-child relationship is inclusive of their children and exclusive of everyone else's children. My children will never feel special in their relationship to me if I insist that they mean no more to me than the neighbor's kids. The same is true in marriage. A healthy marriage requires recognizing who is "in" and who is "out" of the relationship. People who cannot tell the difference become adulterers.

Relationships that are strong and healthy are all "closed" to some degree. In fact, those who boast that they have an "open" relationship are simply admitting that they do not have much of a relationship at all. The deeper a relationship goes, the more closed it becomes, and the more closed it becomes, the closer it becomes. This is a fact of human existence, and to deny it is to deny reality.

The point here is that the human body and its physical appearance was created to be an instrument of intimacy, specifically an instrument of the sexual relationship that celebrates and communicates the covenantal unity of marriage. Sex was designed to make a man and woman one in both body and spirit, thus actualizing the contractual and legal union effected in holy matrimony.

Sex was created to facilitate intimacy, to enact it and enable it, and this intimacy is manifested physically in the glory of covenantal nakedness and the private celebration of physical beauty and attraction that occurs in the secret chamber of a married man and woman.

This is why fornication is so deeply dissatisfying and requires ever-increasingly bizarre experimentation. Sex without covenant acts out a lie. Married sexual relations actualize marital oneness, and thus, fornication has nothing to offer but the empty bodily actions of a sick charade. Fornication is a farce.

So, the nakedness of the body was created to facilitate intimacy. God designed the naked body to arouse the sexual passions that make two people one. Nakedness is an invitation, a powerful, primal call, to enter into the secret places of the body and share oneness of soul.

Thus, when we expose our nakedness to the general public by dressing immodestly, we confuse both our psyche and the psyche of the beholder by issuing an invitation we likely have no intention of fulfilling. When we undress in public, we frustrate intimacy. We reveal the secrets of our body to everyone, and we all know what happens to a relationship when someone breaks a confidence and tells all your secrets.

Immodesty makes intimacy more elusive. Immodesty shares the secrets of the body with total strangers, and this means that there is less for the husband and wife to share exclusively. This causes deep angst within the human psyche that is often unrecognized and contributes to the ongoing dissatisfaction that characterizes the average couple's love life. Immodesty is live, public pornography, and it has exactly the same soul-numbing effect on the love life. When intimacy is lost, love is lost.

There is something very troubling happening to the human race. We are having great difficulty loving because we have trouble keeping secrets. We have real problems with intimacy. We know very little these days about what it means to share in covenantal exclusivity. A planet full of psychiatrists will never be able to sort out the damage that is being done to our daughters and wives as lecherous fathers and husbands encourage their women to display in public the treasures of physical beauty that God gave for a husband to enjoy alone. When a man encourages his wife to expose her body, he is telling her that she is worth very little to him—so little, in fact, that he is willing for the man on the street to share her secret beauty, the beauty that was given by God to facilitate sexual oneness.

Now, I should say here that I am not against women being beautiful and displaying that beauty for all to see. In fact, we shall consider a separate chapter on Modesty and Beauty to further elaborate this point. The Word of God goes to great lengths in various places to show us the beauty of many leading women of scripture, and the bride of Christ is a woman of eternal and spectacular beauty. No, I am not condemning beauty. For all those who equate holiness with homeliness, I am not on your bandwagon.

Rather, what I am referring to is the public display of the parts of the body that are considered to be secret parts and sanctified to the private, priestly love of a godly husband. And this is more than what hides in a bathing suit. Much more.

I once had an awkward experience on an airplane. A very provocatively dressed young woman was seated next to me, and she immediately began telling me that she was a stripper and Playboy model. She told me that she had won Cyber-Playmate of the year. I listened for a few minutes while she told me all this, and then she asked me what I did for a living. I told her I was a pastor. She gasped and sputtered and began apologizing profusely for even mentioning what she did for a living. She was bright red for a bit, and I was grateful that she at least still had the capacity for shame.

We talked for nearly two hours on the flight as I told her about my wife and children and showed her all my pictures. She told me my wife was lovely and that led us to discuss the question of real beauty. In our discussion on beauty, she made the statement that she felt like her beauty should be shared with the world. I responded that her beauty was like gravel on the ground—anyone can pick up gravel and put it in their pocket. Thus, it has no real value. But my wife's beauty, on the other hand, is like diamonds. Because my wife's beauty is for my eyes only, her beauty is rare and valuable. We do not throw diamonds on the ground for anyone to pick up. No, we treasure them and place them in a vault for safekeeping. She confessed that she had never heard it put like that.

Modesty promotes intimacy because modesty recognizes the value of physical beauty and the role that nakedness plays in promoting mental and spiritual health through sexual wholeness in marriage. Modesty declares to the world that both the man and the woman treasure intimacy so much that they will not violate it in deference to worldly fashion. If you are a secret worth keeping, then cover up.

CHAPTER FOUR

MODESTY AND BEAUTY

Modesty and beauty go together. In fact, modesty is an expression of beauty. This overturns one of the prevailing misunderstandings about modesty that homeliness is holiness.

It seems that those who promote modesty often insist on the repression of beauty, especially feminine beauty. In fact, the greatest enforcers of this homeliness code are often females who are themselves repressed. These hardened women are determined that, if they cannot express feminine beauty, no one else will either. It is rather disturbing to see some repress femininity in the name of suppressing vanity and force holiness-minded women into plain, un-frilled, pseudo-masculine hairstyles and clothing just so no hint of beauty may shine through. What in the world would we say if the opposite were being done and men were being required to dress in curls and ruffles to suppress their masculine "vanity"?

The problem here is a deep confusion regarding beauty versus vanity. Scripture says, "Charm is deceitful, and beauty is vain, but a woman who fears the LORD is to be praised." (Proverbs 31:30) However, a closer look at this scripture and the overall biblical witness concerning feminine beauty shows that there is a beauty that is not vain. Just about all of the great matriarchs of the Old Testament are described as physically beautiful. The bride of Christ is a beautiful bride. Beauty is not the problem. Vain beauty is the problem. And vain beauty is vain because it is false. It is false because it is merely external like a bright, artificial smile that disguises dark contempt. True beauty adorns within and without.

True beauty is the beauty that flows from a peaceful spirit. It manifests outwardly in tasteful, well-arranged hairstyles, ornaments and clothing. (I Timothy 2; I Peter 3) In fact, the word "modest" in I Timothy 2 means "well arranged." In I Peter 3, modest apparel is clothing worn without "fear [of] anything that is frightening."

Among other things, Peter is referring to the fear that drives a woman to seek her husband's affection and approval by dressing inappropriately. (See the first part of I Peter 3 where Peter speaks of a woman winning her husband without a word by modest dress and a submitted spirit.) Women are driven by a fear of rejection from lascivious men to dress immodestly in hopes of turning their eye and securing their love. This is a tragic fallacy, and many, many women are broken and embittered by the lie.

Peter teaches that a woman can only overcome this fear by trusting in the Lord that God will give a woman her husband's heart through a submitted and peaceful spirit.

Peter teaches the woman that her faith should be in God, and this faith is expressed in modesty. Immodesty is unbelief.

Peter states, "Do not let your adorning be external—the braiding of hair and the putting on of gold jewelry, or the clothing you wear—but let your adorning be the hidden person of the heart with the imperishable beauty of a gentle and quiet spirit, which in God's sight is very precious." (3:3,4) This is the "imperishable beauty" that does not fade with age. Vain beauty decomposes into decay, but true beauty only increases with age. This is how grandma can be beautiful at eighty-three.

Beauty is elusive. Most women have little understanding of where beauty comes from. They think it comes from a jar or a clothes rack. They think beauty is something they can put on. And this is because the leering, lustful men in their lives have taught them a lie regarding beauty. They have been taught that "sexy is beauty." But this is exactly wrong. Sexiness is fearfulness, the fear that if a woman does not "out-sexy" the other women around her, the man she loves will reject her. In fact, most women dress sexy in order to compete with other women. This is not confidence; this is torment.

I think this is one of the greatest measures of modest apparel: is it sexy or is it beautiful? Does it display the body as a sexual object to be ogled by covenant-breaking men, or does it cover the body as an expression of the decorum and dignity befitting the queen of a godly man's heart? Does the clothing invite the attention of other men in ways that only a husband should be invited, or does the clothing display the glory of a husband and declare that this woman belongs to a covenant-keeping man? Does the clothing ignite lust or inspire respect?

To dress modestly is to dress in appropriate attire. What is fitting apparel to a godly woman who preserves the secret of intimacy with her covenant husband? It is apparel that displays beauty without displaying her body in a sensual way. If we would not have sex in public, then we should not dress sexy in public. As the wise mother once taught her beautiful daughter, we do not advertise what we do not sell. Because sex is a secret between a woman and her covenant husband, she should never dress in a way that whispers her secrets to strangers. Sadly, some women shout their secrets from the housetop.

Chapter Five

Modesty and Glory

In the Bible, to be clothed is to be glorified. And this is more than a metaphor. Clothing really does signify rank and responsibility. Clothing represents position, power and prestige. This is a creational reality that spans all cultures throughout history. Regardless of how primitive or advanced a culture may be, the VIP's will always dress like it.

We all understand, surely, that polite society always develops and defines certain norms and protocols for how we should dress in various occasions depending upon our rank and status. Just offend the sensibilities of polite society by wearing the wrong thing to a party, and you will see. Polite society sometimes is not so polite.

Now, this is not a discussion of what those norms should be. Only that the norms are. My point is that every culture manifests the original created order in this way. To be clothed is to be glorified.

Paul alludes to this idea when he speaks of believers being "clothed upon" with "the house from above," which is the glorified body. Mixed metaphors notwithstanding, Paul does not speak of being glorified in terms of being set free from the bothersome constraints of clothing to run in glorious nakedness across the green meadows of heaven. God forbid! Unless the resurrection is going to drastically alter the way most of us look, that simply would not be heaven. At all. No, Paul speaks of glory in terms of being dressed in resplendent robes of righteousness. Thus, being dressed like this manifests glory.

When God created Adam and Eve, He created them to share in His glory. This means that even apart from the process of death as we know it, which came from Adam's fall, man would have gone through a process of transformation from mortality to immortality, from transience to everlasting life, from mundane creatureliness to an "eternal weight of glory." Redemption has not altered man's destiny, but it has reclaimed it. Man was created to share in the glory of God from before the foundation of the world. Salvation by the Cross is not "Plan B."

All this points to the fact that Adam's destiny was to be clothed in the glory of God, and this means, quite literally, that God intended to dress Adam in actual, material garments that would manifest the glory of God. This is apparent by looking to the Book of Revelation at how the glorified saints are clothed in remarkable garments that shine with glory like the radiance of the sun. But we must not get confused here. These garments are still actual clothing, not just beams of light wrapped around naked flesh. God intended clothing from the beginning to be a personal expression of glory. Your clothes are you.

This is why Adam was so ashamed when he realized he had forfeited the glory of God and was left naked before the world. I think he understood in some primal way that his now-obvious nakedness was a sign of his having forfeited the future uniform of his dominion and glory. The loss of clothing was somehow an existential loss of self, of being and substance. Strip a man of his clothing, and he loses a part of his soul. Adam's nakedness symbolized his demotion in rank and responsibility. Thus, Adam was naked and ashamed. We shall discuss more about the shame of nakedness in a later chapter, but the point made here is that Adam's glory would have been manifest in the robe God put on him. Clothing manifests glory.

This means that we should consider the way we dress as Christians. We should consider what clothing is appropriate in various settings and what message our clothing sends. Clothing is an incarnational manifestation of who we are. The way we dress our body reveals our soul. This means that we should dress one way when changing the oil on our car, and another way entirely when going to see the President. Or, most importantly, the King of kings. And it also means we should dress one way in the bedroom and another way altogether at the mall. Clothing manifests glory.

This brings us back to the matter of modesty. Paul teaches us that Christ is the image and glory of God, that man is the image and glory of Christ and that the woman is the image and glory of the man (I Corinthians 11). This means that our clothing must manifest the glory of the one we were created to "image" and glorify. Thus, when a man dresses modestly he is manifesting his rank and responsibility as a son of God. When a woman dresses modestly, she is manifesting the glory of her covenant husband. When a man dresses immodestly, he embarrasses Christ. When a woman dresses immodestly, she embarrasses her husband, even if he is too dumb to know it.

I referred briefly to this point in an earlier chapter, but this idea needs to be considered more closely. The woman who dresses modestly with class and style brings glory to her husband. This is another reason that we insist that modesty does not require ugly clothing. By no means! Modest clothing should be beautiful and fashionable, as long as the fashion is godly. Clothing should be glorious, not drab and dowdy. It should express the vibrant soul of a godly man or woman by colorfully and joyfully displaying their personality and style. Paul commands us to dress with dignity, not dreariness. Clothing manifests glory!

The woman who dresses modestly is portraying her covenant relationship with her husband by displaying her beauty in a covenant-keeping way. Her clothing says she belongs to the man that lovingly wrapped her in such beautiful garments. She declares that she belongs to the man whose glory she displays. But the woman who dresses immodestly and sexy is declaring that she is fair game and open season to all who care to indulge in the forbidden fruit of her body. And if she is not trying to say that, then she should be fined for false advertisement.

Thus, dressing modestly manifests glory, and dressing immodestly brings shame. Some think that immodesty is a sign of liberty, but in reality it is a sign of slavery. In Bible times, when slavery was the norm, princes wore fine garments, and the slaves went about half naked. There is no glory in being a slave. True glory belongs to sons and daughters, to the heirs of the King. And if we are children of the King, we should dress like it.

CHAPTER SIX

MODESTY AND SHAME

Why was Adam ashamed when he realized he was naked? He was not just embarrassed, he was ashamed. The shame of nakedness permeated his being. Why? Answering this question explains a lot about the psychological effects of public nakedness. To put it simply, God never intended for people to be naked outside of the trust formed in covenantal relationship. When people are naked outside of the protection of covenantal love and trust, they feel exposed and vulnerable. And this vulnerability produces shame.

The fact that is often overlooked by those who promote public nakedness as an expression of human liberty and existential freedom is that those who go naked in the streets are not just exposing their body. They are baring their soul. And the soul does not like it. The soul is a timid thing that understands instinctively that it is threatened when exposed apart from and outside covenantal love. Human being, or better yet, human "becoming," requires the security and safety of relationship in order to flourish and realize self-actualization. The soul needs promises and commitments, and when we strip the body naked in public, or even if we just play peek-a-boo with strangers, we are parading our soul and degrading our humanity.

When a tyrant seeks to strip a man or woman of their humanity, he strips them of their clothing. Nakedness is humiliating. Why? Why should the naked man care? Why not just laugh along with the crowd and enjoy the joke? Why do we all wake up in terror when we have "The Dream"? (You know the one!) Because we all know that our clothing is an emblem of our being, of who we are, a material projection of our existential nature. To be stripped of clothing is to surrender a part of our self. This is why the Nazis stripped people who were about to be gunned down into trenches or gassed methodically in the chambers. Why take away their clothing? They were about to be murdered. Why not leave them their last vestige of dignity and let them die fully clothed? Because public nudity is dehumanizing, and the Nazis had to strip the Jews of their humanity. They could not permit them one shred of dignity. This was the only way those butchers could reckon with their own dying conscience. The Jews had to be dehumanized in order to be slaughtered without regret. Nakedness is dehumanizing.

Nakedness is intended to facilitate the union of souls. We undress in the presence of a loved one for the purpose of removing every barrier, both actual and symbolic, between two souls. Those who are made one flesh are made one soul. This is why fornication is such a mockery of human sexuality and such a destroyer of mental health. Fornication is a lie. Two people who are not one make their bodies say that they are. But the soul knows, and it dies a little more every time reality is distorted. It is ashamed. Thus, and we must grasp this point, immodesty perpetrates a fraud upon the public and upon the self by undressing just enough to arouse the senses but not enough to fulfill the soul. Immodest clothing is public foreplay.

Think about this. A young girl is intimidated by the fashionistas into dressing immodestly, and she complies in order to secure the world's approval, to triumph over her female competitors and, hopefully, to attract the cute guy in the corner at the club. But look a little closer at what happens when she is out of the club atmosphere and observed in the bright lights of the real world. Maybe she and her friends stop by Denny's to powder their nose. Watch her as she walks through. She is pulling at her miniskirt, tugging at her blouse, and giggling with embarrassment as she stumbles through on eight-inch heels. What is wrong with her? She is ashamed. Her soul is crying out against being exposed. She was created for glory, but she is living with shame. She may eventually silence her soul and deaden her conscience, but for just a moment we are catching a glimpse into the human condition and the effect that immodesty has on us.

One final point. The world dresses immodestly to gain acceptance. But the acceptance the soul needs is covenantal. The soul needs a relationship, a commitment, to feel secure, and nakedness was created to facilitate this relationship in marriage, which is the deepest relationship known on this side of the resurrection. So, there is tremendous irony here. Our women dress immodestly to gain acceptance, and the only acceptance they find is a temporary, lustful acceptance that is deeply dissatisfying to the soul. They seek acceptance and find rejection. They seek glory and only find shame.

the girls saying, "Look dad!" as they bared their
: the gratification of leering men (should we call
nnially pubescent creatures "men"?). "Look dad,"
Why do these girls feel the need to humiliate their
ıming their dads would have the dignity to be
Why, indeed? I think it is because instinctively,
ıeir psyche, these girls subconsciously understand
immodesty is related to unrequited love. As little
desperately needed the affirmation and security of
er's love, but could not obtain it. They seek
ı through immodesty, and their shame is their
ame.

ıteresting that the Greek word "*porne*" can mean
:" or "female slave." Women who are stripped
the dehumanizing, objectifying gratification of men
ıd no sort of covenantal intimacy in return have
ıced to sexual slavery. They have become mere
mmodity with no value beyond a body barter. The
x trade flourishes in the nightclubs, on the street
ıd even down at the mall, as women sell themselves
ological slavery. Women trade sex for affection, but
:ing defrauded.

ıesty is a socially accepted form of sex trafficking.
vomen show their bodies and sell their souls. They
 The sexual revolution promised freedom through
ty, but as Peter says, "They promise them freedom,
hemselves are slaves of corruption. For whatever
s a person, to that he is enslaved" (II Peter 2:19). It
: Christians to issue an emancipation proclamation
ı and women: put your clothes on and be set free

CHAPTER SEVEN

MODESTY AND INSANITY

One of the most powerful statements on modesty in
scripture is recorded when Jesus cast demons out of the man
from Gedara. After he was healed, the Bible says that he was
"fully clothed and in his right mind." This highlights an idea
that I have suggested several times so far: modesty is a mental
health issue. Public nakedness is a sign of insanity. And this
insanity is both personal and cultural.

Now, I am not simply trying to be provocative here. I
think that immodesty is truly a sign of dehumanization and
the fragmentation of the human psyche. The first thing a man
does when he goes crazy is strip off his clothes and run naked
in the streets. Ask the attendants down at the mental
institution how difficult it is to keep mentally challenged
people dressed. The tendency to lose any sense of modesty
also often accompanies senility and dementia. Modesty is a
function of a well-balanced mind. Of course, there is a sort of
hyper-modesty that is itself an expression of inordinate shame

and is not an indicator of mental well-being, but we must leave that discussion to another chapter.

Modesty is a fundamental part of the "shalom" (peace through wholeness) of human existence. Holistic mental health is expressed in what Paul calls dressing with dignity. "Likewise also that women should adorn themselves in respectable apparel, with modesty and self-control (or, dignity), not with braided hair and gold or pearls or costly attire, but with what is proper for women who profess godliness-with good works" (I Timothy 2:9, 10, comment mine). Being well-put-together in clothing is meant to be an expression of being well-put-together mentally, emotionally and spiritually. Kids should think about this before they dress in tattered and grungy clothing.

I must emphasize the point. Modesty is a fundamental part of the shalom (peace through wholeness) of human existence. Immodesty is a sign of a fragmented psyche, both the personal psyche and the social psyche. Immodesty is a distorted attempt to attract attention by a man or woman that is failing to achieve the intimacy that is so essential to human well-being. Because they lack intimacy with that special someone, they seek intimacy with anyone. Immodesty screams, "Look at me!" But if you could only hear it, a tortured whisper behind the scream murmurs, "Love me, please, somebody love me!"

The next time you see a girl parading her nakedness on public display, you should say a prayer for her. She is hurting. She is empty. She is desperately crying out for intimacy, for love, but she cannot find it. She mostly likely did not receive the full, unconditional love of her father, and now, she cannot seem to find love in the arms of her various sexual

partners and lovers (note the cr
self-centered fornicators "part
seeks love in the lurid stares of
the stares of men she finds des
finds is the inverted, perverted l
are coming apart because her so
one to love her in such a specia
herself as special enough to pre
special intimacy. Lot of special g

As William Struthers argu
Intimacy: How Pornography H
and women who participat
performance are invariably trou
relationships that have affect
Psychologically healthy people s
participate in public sex. The s
naked in the streets. As mention
a form of public pornography. N

Indeed, those who watch
psychologically fragmented. A
covenantal sex, whether porn
always rooted in a deeply frust
self-centered. The root of
relationships, both with God a
unthankful spirit and ungrateful
is unhealthy sexuality.

Back to the idea of imm
unrequited love. Once, while c
night, the TV in the lobby displ
Gone Wild." And it was aptly n
caught my ear (as I did my best

eye!) was
bodies fo
these pe
they said
dads, ass
ashamed
deep in
that thei
girls they
their fat
affirmatic
father's s

It is
"prostitu
naked fo
who inte
been red
human c
human s
corners a
into psyc
they are

Imm
Men and
are slave
promiscu
but they
overcom
is time f
for all m

from the slavery of public nakedness! Be fully clothed and in your right mind. Immodesty is slavery, and slavery is insane.

Two things in conclusion. First, to be fully human is to be fully clothed. To run naked in the streets is inhuman. The image of God is fully revealed in being fully clothed, for God is nowhere depicted as unclothed. Remember, the glory of God is revealed in glorious apparel. Isaiah 6 reveals the glory of God in the fact that He was clothed in majestic robes and His train filled the temple. We must debunk the pagan notion that ideal, pristine human existence involves public nakedness. The Greeks taught us this lie through art and athletics, which is still the two primary means by which deteriorating cultures fall back into the barbarism of immodesty. The museum and the gymnasium have this in common.

Second, when the personal psyche is damaged by immodesty and individual shalom is lost, it affects those standing nearby. Immodesty is not a personal, private matter, as libertarians like to argue. Immodesty is profoundly social. Thus, the decay of the personal psyche causes the decay of the social psyche, the collective mind of society and culture. Immodesty is insanity, and the insanity goes viral. It permeates the collective consciousness of the world, and the degenerative harm done to the individual soul is done to the societal soul, which, in turn, reinforces the collective pressure of the group upon the individual to join in the emperor's parade and celebrate that he has no clothes (our modern version of an old story). Sharing the shame is an attempt to escape the shame, but instead the shame is multiplied, and the world goes crazy.

It is time for Christians to lift up their head and refuse to be intimidated about modesty. We are not the crazy ones here. They are, and we have let the inmates run the asylum long enough. It is time to stop the insanity.

CHAPTER EIGHT

MODESTY AND AUTHORITY

For many people, modesty is merely a cultural convention. Modesty is whatever the current "everyone" thinks it is. Under these guidelines, however, modesty is very fluid and subjective. It is quite possible for these folks to think that the bikini they are wearing is fairly modest. At least, they winsomely argue, I am not wearing a G-string or going topless. And, no doubt, we are glad of that. But if we use this approach, then going topless at the beach is modest as long as everyone thinks so, and as long as we can compare ourselves favorably to the terribly immodest nudists further down the beach. They are wearing nothing, *nothing*, we say, while smugly noting that we are modestly wearing at least next to nothing.

The point is simply this: modesty must be defined biblically in a way that allows us to transfer godly values from one generation to another. We cannot surrender our interpretation of God's law to the fickle whims of man. Now, as noted in the first chapter on "Modesty and Scripture" there may be certain aspects of modesty that are carefully considered and debated among faithful Christians, and there must be some leeway for disagreement within the framework of local church sovereignty, family house rules and personal convictions. We must respect the sincere disagreements of fellow Christians over where certain lines must be drawn without casting an aspersion on their sincerity and love for God.

Not everyone who draws a line differently than I do is doing so because they are worldly. Of course, I think they are wrong because I think I am right. I am strange that way. But my response to them must be one of courtesy and respect, and I must be willing to discuss our differences in a redemptive and biblical manner. If I am not man enough to talk with them face to face about our differences, then I should not talk about them behind their back. It is amazing to me how much the sin of slander, which is the most refined form of murder, is committed in the name of holiness.

We often seem to think that if we can arbitrarily dismiss a man as worldly and "liberal," then we are not required to take his opinions seriously and consider his arguments. For those who are fundamentally insecure in their opinions to start with, this is a convenient way of avoiding the inconsistencies in their arguments. Discredit the man and silence his voice. Then we are not forced to heed the voices in our head. But if we are right in what we believe, we should be willing to cheerfully and courteously discuss our views with those that see things differently. If we are right, then maybe we can win our brother. And if they are right, then maybe we can be corrected by a brother. However, that sort of balance requires a confident honesty that many simply do not have.

Definitions of modesty vary. Yet, there still must be a basic definition of nakedness that can be derived from scripture and established as a baseline for modesty that must not be violated, period. We should be able to agree at least on the basic standard of modesty set forth in the Garden of Eden when God informed Adam that his apron covering still left him naked and ashamed. I have called this the "robe standard": covering the upper arms, covering the torso and back, and covering the thighs completely, which calls for garments below the knee standing or seated. I think most Christians that take modestly seriously would tend to mostly agree that this should be the baseline.

This idea of "baseline" modesty rests on the idea that modesty is defined by God, at least fundamentally, and that God condemns public nakedness as a sin. This means that we must look to the Word of God as our authority on modesty and not to the world around us. Paul states in another context that those who compare themselves among themselves are not wise. This is true with modesty as well. I have read that that the prevailing customs of modesty in Elizabethan England allowed the women to bare their breasts without shame, but the slightest display of an ankle could call a woman's integrity into question. Some say that the Queen herself would sit on the throne with her breasts exposed. But God forbid she should show an ankle!

It seems to me that this all gets really subjective really quick if we do not hold to Scripture as our authority. And even scripture shows some cultural variation in customs of dress. This is why I think we should go back to the Garden of Eden and use the "robe standard" as the baseline. No doubt this could be disputed, but I think it is a reasonable approach to settling the question of what God defines as nakedness. At least, it seems better to me than allowing the world to define modesty for us.

However, the point that I am really attempting to grasp here with both hands is the connection between modesty and authority. And this idea presses on my mind in two ways. First, modesty is a matter of authority as outlined above. Modesty must be defined in an authoritative manner from and by Scripture. But, second, modesty is itself a matter of authority, and I will close with this, to wax preachy.

I noted in an earlier chapter that Paul discusses head coverings in terms of headship, which has to do with the flow of authority from God to Christ to man to woman. (I Corinthians 11) The "head" here is a metaphor for "source." Though Paul is discussing head coverings and not clothing per se, the connection here between authority and covering relates to the idea of modesty. To be covered in scripture is to be brought under the canopy of protection and authority. We see this in the story of Boaz and Ruth. When a man takes a woman into covenant relationship, he brings her under his covering, both metaphorically and actually. He covers her in his bed, and he covers her when she leaves his bed with beautiful clothing that displays his glory upon her.

We symbolize this in our modern weddings with a bridal veil, though we rarely understand what we symbolize these days. The woman is ushered down the aisle by her father, and the veil she wears represents his authority and government, which has provided her covenantal covering since birth. But now, her father is giving her in marriage to her husband. So, the husband lifts the veil, which is a sign of the removal of the father's covering over his daughter, the end of his

Chapter Seven

Modesty and Insanity

One of the most powerful statements on modesty in scripture is recorded when Jesus cast demons out of the man from Gedara. After he was healed, the Bible says that he was "fully clothed and in his right mind." This highlights an idea that I have suggested several times so far: modesty is a mental health issue. Public nakedness is a sign of insanity. And this insanity is both personal and cultural.

Now, I am not simply trying to be provocative here. I think that immodesty is truly a sign of dehumanization and the fragmentation of the human psyche. The first thing a man does when he goes crazy is strip off his clothes and run naked in the streets. Ask the attendants down at the mental institution how difficult it is to keep mentally challenged people dressed. The tendency to lose any sense of modesty also often accompanies senility and dementia. Modesty is a function of a well-balanced mind. Of course, there is a sort of hyper-modesty that is itself an expression of inordinate shame and is not an indicator of mental well-being, but we must leave that discussion to another chapter.

Modesty is a fundamental part of the "shalom" (peace through wholeness) of human existence. Holistic mental health is expressed in what Paul calls dressing with dignity. "Likewise also that women should adorn themselves in respectable apparel, with modesty and self-control (or, dignity), not with braided hair and gold or pearls or costly attire, but with what is proper for women who profess godliness-with good works" (I Timothy 2:9, 10, comment mine). Being well-put-together in clothing is meant to be an expression of being well-put-together mentally, emotionally and spiritually. Kids should think about this before they dress in tattered and grungy clothing.

I must emphasize the point. Modesty is a fundamental part of the shalom (peace through wholeness) of human existence. Immodesty is a sign of a fragmented psyche, both the personal psyche and the social psyche. Immodesty is a distorted attempt to attract attention by a man or woman that is failing to achieve the intimacy that is so essential to human well-being. Because they lack intimacy with that special someone, they seek intimacy with anyone. Immodesty screams, "Look at me!" But if you could only hear it, a tortured whisper behind the scream murmurs, "Love me, please, somebody love me!"

The next time you see a girl parading her nakedness on public display, you should say a prayer for her. She is hurting. She is empty. She is desperately crying out for intimacy, for love, but she cannot find it. She mostly likely did not receive the full, unconditional love of her father, and now, she cannot seem to find love in the arms of her various sexual partners and lovers (note the cruel irony of calling terminally self-centered fornicators "partners" and "lovers"). So she seeks love in the lurid stares of lecherous men, specifically in the stares of men she finds desirable. But the only love she finds is the inverted, perverted love called "lust." Her clothes are coming apart because her soul is coming apart. She has no one to love her in such a special way that makes her treasure herself as special enough to preserve her special beauty for a special intimacy. Lot of special going on right there.

As William Struthers argues in his book, "Wired for Intimacy: How Pornography Hijacks the Male Brain," men and women who participate in pornographic sexual performance are invariably troubled individuals with broken relationships that have affected their mental well-being. Psychologically healthy people simply do not feel the urge to participate in public sex. The same is true of those who run naked in the streets. As mentioned before, immodesty is itself a form of public pornography. Nakedness is foreplay.

Indeed, those who watch pornography are themselves psychologically fragmented. A lust for anonymous, non-covenantal sex, whether pornography or prostitution, is always rooted in a deeply frustrated psyche that is radically self-centered. The root of pornography is broken relationships, both with God and others, flowing out of an unthankful spirit and ungrateful heart. Autonomous sexuality is unhealthy sexuality.

Back to the idea of immodesty as an expression of unrequited love. Once, while checking in at a hotel late at night, the TV in the lobby displayed a program called "Girls Gone Wild." And it was aptly named. One of the things that caught my ear (as I did my best to keep it from catching my eye!) was the girls saying, "Look dad!" as they bared their bodies for the gratification of leering men (should we call these perennially pubescent creatures "men"?). "Look dad," they said. Why do these girls feel the need to humiliate their dads, assuming their dads would have the dignity to be ashamed? Why, indeed? I think it is because instinctively, deep in their psyche, these girls subconsciously understand that their immodesty is related to unrequited love. As little girls they desperately needed the affirmation and security of their father's love, but could not obtain it. They seek affirmation through immodesty, and their shame is their father's shame.

It is interesting that the Greek word *"porne"* can mean "prostitute" or "female slave." Women who are stripped naked for the dehumanizing, objectifying gratification of men who intend no sort of covenantal intimacy in return have been reduced to sexual slavery. They have become mere human commodity with no value beyond a body barter. The human sex trade flourishes in the nightclubs, on the street corners and even down at the mall, as women sell themselves into psychological slavery. Women trade sex for affection, but they are being defrauded.

Immodesty is a socially accepted form of sex trafficking. Men and women show their bodies and sell their souls. They are slaves. The sexual revolution promised freedom through promiscuity, but as Peter says, "They promise them freedom, but they themselves are slaves of corruption. For whatever overcomes a person, to that he is enslaved" (II Peter 2:19). It is time for Christians to issue an emancipation proclamation for all men and women: put your clothes on and be set free from the slavery of public nakedness! Be fully clothed and in your right mind. Immodesty is slavery, and slavery is insane.

Two things in conclusion. First, to be fully human is to be fully clothed. To run naked in the streets is inhuman. The image of God is fully revealed in being fully clothed, for God is nowhere depicted as unclothed. Remember, the glory of God is revealed in glorious apparel. Isaiah 6 reveals the glory of God in the fact that He was clothed in majestic robes and His train filled the temple. We must debunk the pagan notion that ideal, pristine human existence involves public nakedness. The Greeks taught us this lie through art and athletics, which is still the two primary means by which deteriorating cultures fall back into the barbarism of immodesty. The museum and the gymnasium have this in common.

Second, when the personal psyche is damaged by immodesty and individual shalom is lost, it affects those standing nearby. Immodesty is not a personal, private matter, as libertarians like to argue. Immodesty is profoundly social. Thus, the decay of the personal psyche causes the decay of the social psyche, the collective mind of society and culture. Immodesty is insanity, and the insanity goes viral. It permeates the collective consciousness of the world, and the degenerative harm done to the individual soul is done to the societal soul, which, in turn, reinforces the collective pressure of the group upon the individual to join in the emperor's parade and celebrate that he has no clothes (our modern version of an old story). Sharing the shame is an attempt to escape the shame, but instead the shame is multiplied, and the world goes crazy.

It is time for Christians to lift up their head and refuse to be intimidated about modesty. We are not the crazy ones here. They are, and we have let the inmates run the asylum long enough. It is time to stop the insanity.

CHAPTER EIGHT

MODESTY AND AUTHORITY

For many people, modesty is merely a cultural convention. Modesty is whatever the current "everyone" thinks it is. Under these guidelines, however, modesty is very fluid and subjective. It is quite possible for these folks to think that the bikini they are wearing is fairly modest. At least, they winsomely argue, I am not wearing a G-string or going topless. And, no doubt, we are glad of that. But if we use this approach, then going topless at the beach is modest as long as everyone thinks so, and as long as we can compare ourselves favorably to the terribly immodest nudists further down the beach. They are wearing nothing, *nothing*, we say, while smugly noting that we are modestly wearing at least next to nothing.

The point is simply this: modesty must be defined biblically in a way that allows us to transfer godly values from one generation to another. We cannot surrender our interpretation of God's law to the fickle whims of man. Now, as noted in the first chapter on "Modesty and Scripture" there may be certain aspects of modesty that are carefully considered and debated among faithful Christians, and there must be some leeway for disagreement within the framework of local church sovereignty, family house rules and personal convictions. We must respect the sincere disagreements of fellow Christians over where certain lines must be drawn without casting an aspersion on their sincerity and love for God.

Not everyone who draws a line differently than I do is doing so because they are worldly. Of course, I think they are wrong because I think I am right. I am strange that way. But my response to them must be one of courtesy and respect, and I must be willing to discuss our differences in a redemptive and biblical manner. If I am not man enough to talk with them face to face about our differences, then I should not talk about them behind their back. It is amazing to me how much the sin of slander, which is the most refined form of murder, is committed in the name of holiness.

We often seem to think that if we can arbitrarily dismiss a man as worldly and "liberal," then we are not required to take his opinions seriously and consider his arguments. For those who are fundamentally insecure in their opinions to start with, this is a convenient way of avoiding the inconsistencies in their arguments. Discredit the man and silence his voice. Then we are not forced to heed the voices in our head. But if we are right in what we believe, we should be willing to cheerfully and courteously discuss our views with those that see things differently. If we are right, then maybe we can win our brother. And if they are right, then maybe we can be corrected by a brother. However, that sort of balance requires a confident honesty that many simply do not have.

Definitions of modesty vary. Yet, there still must be a basic definition of nakedness that can be derived from scripture and established as a baseline for modesty that must not be violated, period. We should be able to agree at least on the basic standard of modesty set forth in the Garden of Eden when God informed Adam that his apron covering still left him naked and ashamed. I have called this the "robe standard": covering the upper arms, covering the torso and back, and covering the thighs completely, which calls for garments below the knee standing or seated. I think most Christians that take modestly seriously would tend to mostly agree that this should be the baseline.

This idea of "baseline" modesty rests on the idea that modesty is defined by God, at least fundamentally, and that God condemns public nakedness as a sin. This means that we must look to the Word of God as our authority on modesty and not to the world around us. Paul states in another context that those who compare themselves among themselves are not wise. This is true with modesty as well. I have read that that the prevailing customs of modesty in Elizabethan England allowed the women to bare their breasts without shame, but the slightest display of an ankle could call a woman's integrity into question. Some say that the Queen herself would sit on the throne with her breasts exposed. But God forbid she should show an ankle!

It seems to me that this all gets really subjective really quick if we do not hold to Scripture as our authority. And even scripture shows some cultural variation in customs of dress. This is why I think we should go back to the Garden of Eden and use the "robe standard" as the baseline. No doubt this could be disputed, but I think it is a reasonable approach to settling the question of what God defines as nakedness. At least, it seems better to me than allowing the world to define modesty for us.

However, the point that I am really attempting to grasp here with both hands is the connection between modesty and authority. And this idea presses on my mind in two ways. First, modesty is a matter of authority as outlined above. Modesty must be defined in an authoritative manner from and by Scripture. But, second, modesty is itself a matter of authority, and I will close with this, to wax preachy.

I noted in an earlier chapter that Paul discusses head coverings in terms of headship, which has to do with the flow of authority from God to Christ to man to woman. (I Corinthians 11) The "head" here is a metaphor for "source." Though Paul is discussing head coverings and not clothing per se, the connection here between authority and covering relates to the idea of modesty. To be covered in scripture is to be brought under the canopy of protection and authority. We see this in the story of Boaz and Ruth. When a man takes a woman into covenant relationship, he brings her under his covering, both metaphorically and actually. He covers her in his bed, and he covers her when she leaves his bed with beautiful clothing that displays his glory upon her.

We symbolize this in our modern weddings with a bridal veil, though we rarely understand what we symbolize these days. The woman is ushered down the aisle by her father, and the veil she wears represents his authority and government, which has provided her covenantal covering since birth. But now, her father is giving her in marriage to her husband. So, the husband lifts the veil, which is a sign of the removal of the father's covering over his daughter, the end of his administration and government over her, the end of his protection and provision for her, and the beginning of the newly-wed husband's covering and authority. The removal of the veil is a sign of a change in government.

After the veil is lifted, the groom kisses the bride, which is the first fruits of intercourse, and he takes her to his chamber where he uncovers her to discover the secrets of her love, and their covenantal nakedness is glorious and beautiful. But the husband does not leave his bride uncovered and parade her naked through the streets. Rather, he wraps her in the garments of his protection and provision. He clothes her in glory. God speaks this way in the prophets about His marriage to Israel.

This symbolism is found throughout scripture. Clothing represents position and power. To be covered is to possess authority. To be stripped naked is to be enslaved. There are several examples of this. Joseph's coat of many colors was not just a fancy suit. It was the uniform of stewardship and authority over Jacob's house. His trip to find his brothers was an audit of their business on their father's behalf. When his brothers stripped him of his coat, they robbed him of his authority.

The Prodigal Son was clothed in the garments of sonship when he returned home. The saints are clothed in garments of righteousness in the resurrection, which is sign of the investiture of authority and dominion in the world to come. We understand this very well in our own world. There are various social orders within our world, such as the military, police and public service departments, etc., that recognize authority through clothing. The authority does not reside within the clothing, but the clothing manifests it.

Also, torn, or rent, clothing in scripture represents the loss of authority. When Saul tore Samuel's garment, it was a sign that the kingdom had been rent from him. When the High Priest rent his garment, which he was forbidden to do by the Law of Moses, at Jesus' trial before the Sanhedrin, he was symbolizing the end of his priesthood without knowing it. The prophetic imagery of "rending the heavens" throughout the Old Testament symbolizes the fall of governments. When the king of Ammon cut off the garments of David's ambassadors just below their buttocks, he rejected their authority as illegitimate by humiliating them with public nakedness. The Law of Moses commanded the men who took female captives of war to be their wives to remove the "raiment of her captivity" as a sign of the forsaking of past relationships and authority. (Deuteronomy 21:13)

The point here is that modest clothing is more than just a matter of personal dignity, though it is certainly that. Modest clothing manifests authority, both the authority that covers us, and the authority with which we cover others. When our clothes are rent and our nakedness is exposed, we are demonstrating a breakdown in authority. We are manifesting both insubordination to authority and abdication of authority. We are defying and denying authority at the same time.

Immodesty is instinctively understood to be an expression of rebellion against authority. This is why immodest girls are described as "wild." And they are not just resisting social norms. The immodestly dressed young woman is defying her father's authority, whether or not he or she knows it. Moreover, she is defying her future husband's authority by displaying her secret beauty to anyone who happens to be looking on.

If Christians intend to exercise in earth the dominion that Christ wields in heaven, which is what we are taught to pray every day ("Thy kingdom come. Thy will be done in earth as it is in heaven."), then we must see the incarnational connection between the way we dress and the way we rule. We must understand that immodesty is a forfeiture of dominion. If we wish to speak to this world with authority and as authorities on living the abundant life, we must do so from the standpoint of living under authority. And that is exemplified in the way we dress.

We must be willing to model the order we propose in the gospel. It is no accident that the word translated "modest" in Paul's writing is the Greek word "*cosmeo*," which means orderly and well-arranged. If we plan to change the "cosmos," the world in which we live, then we must embody "cosmeo" in the way we dress. "Cosmeo" is first seen in our modest clothing. Appropriate attire is authoritative attire.

CHAPTER NINE

MODESTY AND FEMINISM

For some, modesty is seen as a form of patriarchal oppression. Since rules of modesty are nearly always focused more on women than men, requirements for modesty in whatever form, whether rigid rules or even simple discussions such as this, are often seen as expressions of misogynist chauvinism. The right to undress in public is seen by some as essential to feminine self-expression, and any man who states otherwise hates women. Simple as that. For many, nakedness is an ownership issue, as with the related issue of abortion, and women must be free to control their own body without interference. "No one has the right to tell me what to do with my body!" This is the dogma that the sexual revolution taught us.

And the old hippie dogmatists are correct that nakedness is an ownership issue. Indeed, this has been one of the assumptions I have worked from so far. But no one owns their body or soul alone. Human being is a partnership. All parental and marital relations involve mutual ownership. Life is never a sole proprietorship, no matter how much we boast about our independence. As Paul tells us, no lives or dies unto himself. We are all connected.

The idea of mutual ownership may be controversial in these days of radical individualism, but in the Bible it is accepted as a given idea. Paul states without a hint of stuttering embarrassment in I Corinthians 7 that the husband owns the wife and the wife owns the husband. This idea is why he can speak of adultery in I Thessalonians 4 as "defrauding" a brother. A wife belongs to her husband, a husband belongs to his wife. And their nakedness, which is as much a prelude to sex as a romantic hug or kiss, also belongs to one another. If no decent man would ever approve of his wife sharing a kiss with strangers, then he should never accept her sharing her nakedness with strangers. A man who steals a peek is much like the man who steals a kiss. Both men are guilty of grand larceny.

Moreover, unmarried girls belong to their parents until they are "given in marriage," an old biblical phrase that is deeply offensive to modern sensibilities, but is still deeply true to human nature and the way God created the world regardless of our petulant protests against it. In the Bible, which reveals the way God created the world and what it means to be human as the image of God, men marry and women are given in marriage. Thus, we all are owned by the relationships that define our personal identity. I am a son, a husband and a father. These are aspects of who I am. I cannot be me apart from these aspects of me. Thus, I am owned existentially. I cannot escape it. This means that my body belongs to those who own me. I cannot do what I want with myself by myself. For example, if I become addicted to drugs or alcohol, I affect profoundly and negatively everyone connected with me. I am connected whether or not I like it. Mutual ownership of self is simply a fact of human existence. So, the feminists were right that nakedness is an ownership issue, but they were wrong about who owns it.

However, this idea of modesty as misogynist repression is exactly backwards. It is actually immodesty that represses women and turns them into dehumanized objects of leering male lust. When men treat women this way, without a grain of respect for them as a person, as nothing more than an object to be ogled or a live sex toy to be handled, then the humanity of the woman as a woman – in other words, her existential feminine persona – is degraded. She is not just being degraded as a human; she is being degraded specifically as a woman. The strip clubs mostly want women to strip. This exploitation should outrage true feminists.

Moreover, immodesty has deeply affected feminine self-esteem. From movie stars to swimsuit models, from the runways of Paris to the halls of the local high school, the modern immodesty ethos has pornographized our culture and forced our girls to believe that they must look like Barbie to be beautiful. Immodesty has put unbelievable pressure on our girls to keep their weight down unnaturally and their figure reduced unhealthily so that they can look sexy in a bathing suit. Breast implants, tummy tucks, and now, of all things, buttock implants, are tragic indications of a deeply disturbed feminine psyche. And it is the men that have done the deep disturbing.

Women feel like they must keep their eighteen-year-old body, even after they have been married ten years and have birthed three children, in order to keep their husband's interest. Men and women that should be cheerfully growing old and saggy together without a twinge of embarrassment have been deceived to think they cannot be sexually fulfilled if they are not chock full of silicone, collagen and Botox. Come on, Grandma! Grow old gracefully. When will we say that enough is enough and stop the madness? We are destroying our wives and daughters. And it all begins with enculturated immodesty that strips our women of their self-esteem.

So, ironically, it is modesty that best reveals femininity. Modesty celebrates femininity. It celebrates women as women, as full persons and not just as bodies to be gawked at and groped after. The feminine spirit attains its fullness in the context of covenantally faithful and self-respecting modesty. Thus, true feminism, the sort of feminism that actually loves what is womanly about women and does not seek to subjugate women as either caricatured, soulless sex objects or de-feminized pseudo-males, should promote modesty as self-actualizing for women and cut out the foolishness of encouraging young women to discover their feminine self by uncovering their female body.

Immodesty is unloving and unloved. The woman who dresses immodestly is not showing love, for others or for herself, and the man who ogles the immodestly dressed woman is not giving love. As C.S. Lewis said about prostitution, a man does not love the woman he pays for sex. She is simply the "necessary apparatus" required for his sexual gratification. The man cares nothing for her, for her children or her deepest needs and desires. She is just an object to be used, paid and thrown away. In fact, she is paid so she can be thrown away, so that no further obligation is expected. Douglas Wilson remarks that these men love women like little boys love ice cream. Just something to be tasted and devoured for selfish pleasure. Everybody scream for ice cream!

The cultural compulsion toward female public nakedness is a form of male dominance over women. It was men that dreamed this up. And quite a dream it was! Dissolute men have enculturated a so-called feminist philosophy of sexual liberation in order to get women comfortable with undressing in public. And the women went for it. What a deal! The men who first developed and articulated feminist philosophy – and have no doubt, it was men who first did so – went to great academic and intellectual lengths to persuade ordinary women to bare their bodies in public. And their most significant achievement was to convince the ladies that they thought of it.

Modesty empowers women. It does so because modesty is closely aligned with monogamy, and monogamy provides the greatest framework for enduring feminine influence. George Gilder in his book, "Men and Marriage," discusses the significant social power that women have with men when they require them to marry them and provide for their children in order to enjoy sexual prerogatives. It is a sign of feminine strength when a girl insists on marriage before sex. This sort of girl is saying in so many words that she is worth a lifetime.

Gilder shows that social order breaks down when women give men the sex they want without demanding covenantal faithfulness in marriage. When women undress themselves for public display and sleep with men outside of marriage, they are surrendering their primal power in society. They have the ability to tame the animal urge within men, as Gilder describes it, by domesticating them. This is why rape is such a universal outrage. Rape strips a woman of her natural right to say no, and when that right is lost, the fabric of human society comes apart. Modesty empowers women, and women empower the world. Whoever said it is a man's world must not have had a mother.

Moreover, modesty provides protection for women. Modesty is a protective covering, both physically and spiritually. Immodesty makes women more vulnerable to predatory men, and I do not mean this in the sense of the old canard that scantily dressed women are to blame for being raped. Not at all. But it is true that modesty protects women from invasive stares. No doubt some men will stare if a woman is dressed from head to toe in a hazmat suit. But all men will tend to stare when a woman is hardly dressed at all. Modesty protects women.

These ideas of power and protection come together in the practice of modesty. When women accept the false premise that female liberation requires immodesty and immorality, then the tyranny of patriarchy, such as seen in Islamic societies, is replaced by the tyranny of pimps and playboys, such as seen on MTV. Either way, the women lose. The men rule, and the women are enslaved. Unscrupulous men, understanding that men look to lust and women lust to be looked at, exploit the feminine need for male acceptance and the vulnerability of women's natural desire to be attractive, and their women are reduced down to common property in a public harem. This is not freedom, and neither is it genuine feminism. It is slavery.

Enculturated immodesty is a form of sexual abuse. And again, I am not seeking to be provocative, nor am I trivializing sexual abuse. I mean to say, and say it charitably, yet boldly, that persuading women to overcome their natural urge to cover their bodies is a form of sexual aggression forced on them by lecherous men. Most women can describe the extreme discomfort of being visually undressed by some creep at the mall or some other public place. But these days, the creeps have won, the women have given in and immodesty is expected – nay, demanded! – of our girls.

Then, the fathers and husbands who resist this lechery by advocating modesty are accused of being patriarchal chauvinists that seek to oppress women in an outdated, Victorian past (which, by the way, is as much a myth as the myth of repressed Puritan sexuality). Nonsense! Rather, these advocates of modesty simply respect women as women and rise courageously to their defense. Women who are surrounded by men like these are women who live within the security of godly protection and exercise the power of extended and enduring female influence. Who is more empowered and secure, the "hot" stripper dancing naked around the pole, or a dowdy grandmother gathering three or four loving generations around her table?

Allow me to conclude with one final thing. It is true that some have taken modesty too far and actually oppressed women under the guise of teaching modesty through overbearing dress standards, though, oddly enough, it is nearly always the women in these oppressive cultures who are the harshest enforcers of the uniform code. There may be nothing quite as vicious as a pack of females attacking another woman that dares to flout the rules. Examples of modesty-distortion would be Amish-style clothing, the dress standards of some radical holiness movements and, most extreme of all, the burka required by some Islamic societies. In reality, this sort of pride-driven modesty is not modesty at all, and we repudiate these extremes.

However, just because some have distorted the idea of modesty and abused women as a result, does not mean that all teaching on modesty is legalistic patriarchalism. Those who equate the two simply have not worked all the way through the implications of their position. Although, speaking of working your way through the implications, I was tickled the other day (I probably should have been more outraged than amused, but I couldn't muster up the indignation) to read one critic of teaching on modesty say that he would not be offended if Christians chose to visit nude beaches and sunbathe in the buff as long as they did not feel condemned by it. Now, either this gentleman is profoundly naive concerning both the human condition and the teaching of Scripture, or he has other reasons for encouraging the freedom to visit nude beaches that the Lord will have to judge. Either way, we are forced to give him kudos for consistency! But, sadly, in an attempt to avoid being judgmental, some sincere Christians fail to exercise good judgment.

No doubt we must insist on discerning the difference between biblical modesty and legalistic modesty, and we shall consider this more closely in a moment. But for now we must strongly object to those who equate modesty with female oppression. In fact, we insist that immodesty is a form of female oppression just as much as overbearing legalism. Both are imposed by profligate men to subjugate women. The bikini is just as oppressive as the burka.

CHAPTER TEN

MODESTY AND LEGALISM

One of the most common objections raised against teaching on modesty is that it is "legalistic." And this a valid concern, though, as we shall see, it often misses the point by attempting to tweezer a splinter while impaled on a pole. But we should grant freely and truthfully that much teaching on modesty is indeed driven by a legalistic impulse. This failing should confronted and confessed, and we should seek assiduously to avoid it. Or, carefully and persistently, if you prefer. Those of us who strongly emphasize a message of separation from the world do holiness doctrine no favors when we refuse to repent for the self-righteousness that tries to make Pharisees out of us all.

So, let us admit it. Much of our teaching on modesty is driven by the attempt to produce righteousness through external law-keeping. We tend to think we can make people modest if we make them dress modest. But this is an oft-demonstrated fallacy. Modest dress is often the best disguise for an immodest spirit. When a young woman climbs in the backseat of her boyfriend's car and removes her long skirt and high-necked blouse in order to better facilitate adolescent hanky-panky, she demonstrates that modesty doesn't come at all from the way we dress. It comes from the heart. But she also demonstrates that modesty determines the way we dress – or, undress, in this instance. Modesty may not begin on the outside, but it will certainly end up on the outside. Sort of like fruit on a tree.

However, legalistic holiness teaching gets the fruit all mixed up with the root, and, as any amateur horticulturist will tell you, this is a serious mistake. Quite serious. Getting the fruit and the root mixed up will have you aerating apples and pruning the ground. Simply will not work. But we often try it. We think we can make people holy if we simply teach them the rules. But, speaking of apples, this is the original sin, the attempt to be holy by learning the rules. This was Adam's mistake. He tried to become godly, "like God," by choosing the tree of law over the tree of life. It did not work.

Adam and Eve believed Satan's lie that they could be holy by simply learning to discern good and evil. Of course, discernment of good and evil is a good thing in the right context. Hebrews 5 tells us that discernment is the true mark of Christian maturity. But Adam sought discernment apart from relationship with God. He thought he could be holy simply by learning the rules. This is the first instance of legalism, and we still wrestle with it today. So, it is true that teaching on modesty often short-circuits the grace of God that imparts true holiness from within by choosing the quick and easy route of simply dressing up hypocrites with uniform standards.

So, let me say it again. Much of our teaching on modesty is indeed driven by this sort of legalism. And yet, now that I have admitted it, drawing applause from liberals and stirring suspicion from conservatives, let me add that just because something is taught in a legalistic way does not make it wrong. We can forbid adultery in a legalistic way, but that does not make adultery okay. Just so, the fact that the critics of holiness teaching can truthfully object that much teaching on modesty is legalistic does not *ipso facto* prove teaching on modesty wrong. No, just that it is being taught in the wrong way. This is a great mystery that requires much careful consideration. Selah.

Yet, while we are eagerly condemning legalism, I must point out that there are two ways to be legalistic. Herein lies another great mystery. Legalism has two forms, a "conservative" form, with which we are all familiar, and a "liberal" form, with which we are less familiar because it is so cleverly disguised as "Christian liberty." Liberal legalism is even more insidious than conservative legalism because it is less decried and thus less obvious.

In order to grasp this point, we must remember that legalism is, according to my handy-dandy dictionary, "strict conformity to the letter of the law rather than its spirit." Think about this now. Strict conformity to the letter of the law can occur negatively as well as positively. In other words, those who rigorously point to the absence of law, which they equate with Christian liberty, as proof they are not required to do a certain thing are just as law-oriented as the person who rigorously points to the presence of law demanding certain actions. Both end up relying on the law for justification. One says that we are required to do such and so because the law says so and thinks he is saved as a result of his careful allegiance to the rules. The other says that he is required to do no such a thing, thank you very much, because you cannot show me a law that says I have to. So there.

Both of these folks are governed by law rather than love. Both are legalists. There are some things for which there simply is no law. Like, love, joy, peace, etc., the fruit of the Spirit: "Against such things there is no law." (Galatians 5:23) But love requires that we seek the good of our neighbor even when there is no explicit law. And this should be what drives our teaching on modesty. We should seek to manifest love in the way we dress.

This is an important point for the discussion on modesty. Those who point to the absence of any explicit commandment defining what modesty means are still law-oriented in their quest for justification. This is legalism. We must go beyond this legalistic approach and seek a Spirit-led interpretation and application of scripture for these uncertain issues. And because we must be led by the Spirit in deciphering inexplicit principles of scripture, we must afford one another some reasonable leeway in working out the details. This is where charity would be quite helpful.

In conclusion, please allow me to emphasize that I am sincerely seeking a definition of modesty from scripture based on its overall witness from Genesis to Revelation. This is why I point to the coats with which God clothed Adam as the basis for modesty. Their aprons were not enough. This what I have called "the robe standard." This is also why I have pointed to the robes of the saints in the Book of Revelation as proof that the ultimate destiny of man is to be fully clothed. I want to let scripture define modesty. I have no desire to be legalistic in either the conservative or liberal form.

My point rests on this: God explicitly forbids public nakedness and commands modesty. We are required, then, to deal with this issue. We have three options. First, tradition. Second, culture. Third, scripture. We must choose the third way because the others are legalistic in the sense that they impose or refuse rules apart from Christ.

Of course, it is obvious that scripture does not spell out specifics regarding modesty as clear as the Ten Commandments. But that does not release us from the obligation of seeking to explain modesty scripturally. It simply prohibits us from absolutizing our interpretations in a way that disqualifies differing, sincere opinions. We can work with those who differ with us within reason on how scripture defines modesty, be they more conservative or liberal than we are. What we cannot do is reason faithfully with those who deny the authority and sufficiency of scripture altogether in the name of rejecting legalism. That is antinomianism, pure and simple. But explaining that monster word would require another chapter.

CHAPTER ELEVEN

MODESTY AND WORSHIP

There is a direct connection in scripture between modesty and worship. Or, to put it negatively, there is a direct connection between immodesty and idolatry. In the Bible, the worship of the one true God was necessarily done while clothed in garments for "glory and beauty" (Exodus 28:2) while the worship of idols was often performed in nakedness.

God not only commanded His priests to wear garments for "beauty and glory," but He also commanded them to wear linen undergarments that would "reach from the hip to the thigh" and hide their nakedness when they ministered before Him at the altar (Exodus 28:42). Even when David danced before the Lord and removed His royal robes, which his wife, Michal, sarcastically calls "making yourself naked like a fool," he was covered with the linen ephod that the priests were required to wear in worship. The Law of God is explicit that true worship is expressed in modest clothing.

Pagans, on the other hand, were infamous throughout various cultures for worshipping their gods while stripped naked. In fact, many forms of idol worship throughout the ancient world specifically included sexual deviancy as an expression of perverted worship. The temple of Aphrodite in ancient Corinth had a thousand temple prostitutes to serve the worshippers. Pagan worship included all forms of sexual sins such as homosexuality, pedophilia and bestiality. As far back as the Golden Calf, Israel ended up naked when she imitated the practices of the heathen. (I Corinthians 10:6-11) There is always a direct correlation in scripture and history between idolatry and fornication. Of course, getting naked is the first step toward fornication. Immodesty and idolatry always go together.

In Romans 1, Paul shows us an explicit connection between idolatry and fornication. "Therefore God gave them up in the lusts of their hearts to impurity, to the dishonoring of their bodies among themselves, because they exchanged the truth about God for a lie and worshiped and served the creature rather than the Creator, who is blessed forever! Amen." (Romans 1:24, 25) Improper worship causes man to lose his creational bearings, his natural orientation, and he begins to embody the collapse of his existential identity through sexual perversion. Idolatry leads inexorably to fornication.

When man loses sight of God as His Creator, he loses sight of himself as God's creation, for he is created to be a reflection of God, and humanity becomes inhuman. And inhumane, for that matter. Idolatry leads to a crisis in sexual identity because sexual identity comes from God and can only be properly preserved through right worship. Worship reveals who God is, which reveals who man is. Think about Isaiah beholding the glory of God and responding in terror, "Woe is me! I am lost!" Man sees himself in light of his revelation of God. Idolatry blinds man to himself and leads to the distortion of self that is expressed in sexual sin. Fornication is always a result of idolatry.

The loss of God-centered sexual identity leads to the loss of covenantal sexuality, which is sex in the sanctity of marriage, and the loss of covenantal sexuality leads to public nakedness. Private intimacy becomes public display. When men and women lose sight of God and His holiness—in other words, when they fail to worship—they fixate their gaze on one another. And when they start staring at one another rather than beholding the glory of God, they begin to lust after one another. As Paul says in Colossians, covetousness is idolatry. Lust is worship failure.

When God as the Creator is no longer the center of creation, then the covenantal expression of the one-flesh relationship that God ordained—sex in the sanctity of marriage—becomes a frustrating barrier to self-gratification. The love of God is replaced by the lust of man, and fornication becomes the only way that lustful man can express his pathetically impotent sexual identity. How are the mighty fallen!

Let me say it again. There is a direct connection between modesty and worship. Immodesty is an indication of self-worship, which is the root of all idolatry. Immodesty is an inglorious display of the body in a way that pleads to be worshipped. "Please," Immodesty begs, "look at me! Behold me! Worship me!" When lustful men demand that their women run naked in the streets, they too are promoting self-worship, for they are worshipping the female body in order to gratify their own desires. In fact, they are not really worshipping the woman at all; they are worshipping their own desires. Men look to lust; women lust to be looked at. Idolatry is always a selfish projection of human desires. Idolatry is always rooted in self-worship, the veneration of the body and its passions to the detriment of the soul and its visions. Immodesty is idolatry.

As noted above, God commanded that His priests be dressed modestly when they ministered before Him. This theme is carried out in the New Testament as well. In both places in the New Testament where Paul and Peter talk about modest dress, their teaching is set in the context of priestly worship. Paul writes about the public worship service and commands the men and women to dress modestly as a matter of decorum before God while "lifting up holy hands" (I Timothy 2). Peter addresses the idea of modesty in the larger context of worship in the world as Christians live out their priestly calling in all nations. (I Peter 2, 3) In both instances modesty is taught as a matter of priestly ministry. Modesty is an expression of worship.

In I Corinthians 11, Paul takes the idea of proper attire even further when he teaches the women of Corinth to be covered in worship "because of the angels" (I Corinthians 11:10). There is a wide spectrum of thought on what this means exactly, but, whatever all it means, it at least means that the way we dress in worship is observed by angels and affects their response to us. My point here is simply that decorum in dress is a worship issue. The angels of God take note of how we are dressed and regard it as a matter of preparation for priestly service. As Paul asks, "Is it comely for a woman to pray uncovered?" The way we dress expresses submission to God. Modesty and worship go together.

One final point. If modesty and worship go together, then we must consider where worship occurs so we can know where modesty should occur. Think about it for a moment. Worship happens in the temple of God, and the temple of God exists on three levels: the temple of our bodies, the temple of the church and the temple of the universe. This means that we must dress modestly in private worship, though we exercise the liberty of covenantal nakedness in the marriage bed; we must dress modestly in congregational worship, for we are gathered with the holy saints and angels; and we must dress modestly while ministering in the world wherever we are anywhere in the universe, for our priestly ministry in the world mediates holiness to all creation.

This point of private, congregational and universal priesthood is very important to our discussion. It refutes the idea that modesty should happen only when we go to church. We minister as priests upon the altar wherever we are at all times. We are priests in our homes with our families. We are priests in the church when we gather to worship. And we are priests at the mall and at the beach. Therefore, because we are priests at all times and everywhere we go, we are called to be clothed in righteousness and covered in holiness. Modesty and worship go together.

CHAPTER TWELVE

MODESTY AND NEW CREATION

In this final chapter, I think we should begin by hearkening back to two things that we have brushed by several times as we hurried along. First, man was not created to be naked. He was created to be clothed in glory and beauty. Nakedness was a sign of man's innocence and immaturity, and moreover, the indications of heavenly *haute couture* glimpsed throughout history and in prophetic previews of the resurrection show that man's ultimate destiny is to be properly clothed. God is "robed in righteousness," and man is created to bear His image.

Second, the word rendered "modest" comes from the word "*cosmeo*," from which we derive our English word "cosmetics." The word *cosmeo* is a form of the word "*cosmos*," which means "order." Thus, to dress modestly is to dress appropriately, or in proper order. Both the created world and proper dress styles are described as *cosmos*, as orderly. Thus, scripture draws a straight line between the creation order and modesty. Modesty is endemic to the creation order.

Man was created as the universe in miniature. Or, to put it more exactly, the universe was created to expand and magnify the glory of God revealed in man. Both the body of man and the universe were created to be the temple of God, and as such, both were created to reveal divine order centered in true worship. Man was created according to the three-fold structure of the temple, outer court (body), inner court (soul) and Holy of Holies (spirit). The universe reflects the same pattern: outer court (earth), inner court (the visible heavens) and the Holy of Holies (the heavens beyond the veil where God dwells, the "third heavens"). Thus, the way we dress must display the same sort of order that God etched into the night sky. The heavens declare the glory of God, and so must our clothing.

Now, I am leaning hard on this connection between modesty and creation in order to make the point that modesty is more than cultural accommodation. Modesty is an embodiment of the divine order woven into the warp and woof of the universe. To parade through the streets in nakedness, which seems to me to be best defined by what God covered in Eden, is to strip the temple of its glory. To be modest is to manifest God's creation order.

And, speaking of creation, getting dressed in appropriate attire is reminiscent of the opening days of creation. The Spirit of God brooded over the waters of unformed creation and began by His Word to make cosmos out of chaos. God clothed all creation in glory and beauty and decorated it with magnificent adornment. God dressed the heavens and earth in the garments of priestly worship. This is why the writer can speak of the heavens as garments that shall be changed in the new creation (Hebrews 1:10-12), which is a point that we shall consider in a moment.

In a way, we could say that God's covering of Adam in Eden was a reenactment of creation in miniature, a microcosm of creation. God covered the chaos of nakedness with the order of modest clothing, of well-arranged garments. To return to public nakedness is to revert to the chaos that characterized the barrenness of pre-creation. Indeed, it is no coincidence that godly nakedness, the nakedness of the marriage bed, is a moment of creation when new life is brought out of the womb of water and spirit. Never is man closer to bearing the image and sharing the glory of God than when he performs his imitative role of creating new life. This is why fornication and adultery is such an affront to God. Creation must occur within the boundaries of divine order, within the secret place of a loving covenant. Otherwise, the world spins out of control.

So, modesty is cosmos. Creation was formed to reflect order. However, creation has become disordered through sin and death. In a way, we could say that the garments of creation have become tattered and torn. It is significant that nakedness in scripture is symbolic of man's fall into sin and shame. Just like a woman that has been brutally assaulted and left dying with her garments ripped away, so God's good creation has been violated by Satan and his hordes of demon powers.

Yet, we have a wonderful promise. God will make all things new, which He has already begun in the resurrection of Christ. When new creation comes, the heavens shall be changed like a garment. The nakedness of creation shall be covered in the resurrection glory of new creation. The universe shall put on new clothes.

Therefore, immodesty is an embodiment of chaos and decreation. Modesty is an embodiment of new creation, a foreshadowing of the day when all things shall be made new. When we dress in modest apparel we are modeling the world to come when the nakedness of sin and death will be "clothed upon" with the garments of resurrection glory.

We should never be intimidated to dress modestly. By doing so, we become living placards, walking billboards, as it were, announcing the coming new creation. When we reject the nakedness of pagan culture, we are proclaiming the descent of heaven to earth, as the heavenly city comes down from God out of heaven "adorned as bride for her husband." She has her wedding garments on. To dress modestly is to preach the transcendence of Christian culture and that the church will not be forced into adapting cultural expressions of chaos and decreation. To dress modestly is to declare that we have left the hog pen of prodigal wanderings and have returned to the Father's house to be clothed with the best robes and to wear the kingly ornaments of glory and beauty.

One final point, and this may be one of the most urgent things we have considered. Modesty is an expression of holiness unto the Lord. To dress immodestly is unholy. Yet, we must be careful right here. Modesty is an expression of holiness, but it is not holiness *per se*. Just because we dress modestly does not mean that we are holy. This point must be carefully considered and soaked into the pores of our mind. This distinction must be understood to keep us from becoming like the priest and the Levite in the story of the Good Samaritan. They walked quickly by on the far side of the road because they thought that helping the stranger might defile their purity and contaminate their holiness.

Christians that emphasize modesty often tend to do the same thing. We often wear modesty like an armor to protect us from being contaminated by the world, and the arrogance of this attitude is keenly felt by the world around us. The man at Starbucks wearing the wife-beater shirt and the montage of tattoos knows very well when he is being looked at down the nose. But modesty is not intended to set us apart in a superior way. Rather, modesty is intended to model new creation. Modesty should inspire interest in beauty and glory. As noted early on, holiness is not homeliness. Modesty should be attractive.

Holiness flows out like a river. Holiness is not intended to stay bottled up like an aquarium where enthralled spectators view another world through glass. No, holiness flows out into the world to heal the world. The resurrection of Jesus in the middle of history means that the coming new creation when all things shall be made new in the resurrection has already broken into the world now. Holiness must be a foretaste of the world to come. Thus, modesty must inspire modesty. We must model holiness in such a way that the world longs for new creation like a thirsty man longs for a cool drink of water. Let the river flow!